The Story of Libraries

by Seth Williams

PEARSON

Scott
Foresman

Editorial Offices: Glenview, Illinois • Parsippany, New Jersey • New York, New York
Sales Offices: Needham, Massachusetts • Duluth, Georgia • Glenview, Illinois
Coppell, Texas • Ontario, California • Mesa, Arizona

Around 650 B.C. in ancient Assyria, King Ashurbanipal had just won a war against Babylon. **Prideful** of his place in history, the king took valuable clay tablets from Babylon and added them to his library in Nineveh. In one of the tablets, the king left a message saying that anyone who broke, harmed, or removed the tablet and replaced it would be cursed by the gods.

There was nothing **peculiar** about the king's threat. Books in the ancient world were valuable because of the information they contained. Then, as it is now, knowledge was power. The information in a book could be as powerful as an army.

Early and modern forms of written communication

Early Libraries and the Written Word

The word *library* comes from *liber*, the Latin word for "book." The first books were written by hand on rolls of paperlike material, *papyrus*, around 3000 B.C. Other early books were handwritten on clay tablets from around the same time. Among the first libraries, or record rooms, was a group of tablets dating to around 2300 B.C. that was found near Nippur in Mesopotamia. The tablets listed geographical names, gods, names of professions, and a number of religious hymns.

Tablet writing from around 3000 B.C.

It was the Greeks who developed libraries with books on all subjects available to all readers. But it was not easy. The Dark Age of ancient Greece took place from 1200 B.C. to 900 B.C. During this time cities were destroyed and the knowledge of how to write was lost. Fortunately the Phoenicians, who lived in present-day Lebanon and Israel, had developed a form of writing that was fairly simple to learn. The Greeks adapted letters from this alphabet to make their own alphabet.

By the 400s B.C. the Greeks also had created a way to teach people about different subjects. Poetry and religious works were written down, as well as works in history, art, and even cooking.

Ancient Greek ruins

The Royal Library at Alexandria

The greatest center of ancient civilization in the Middle East was Egypt, home of the famous Royal Library at Alexandria. Founded around 300 B.C. by the Greek king Ptolemy I, it lasted for nearly six hundred years. It was the first library to offer a wide variety of books. It had about half a million handwritten rolls, or scrolls.

The Royal Library at Alexandria

We know this because one man, Callimachus, put together an index of the entire library's writings telling about each piece of work. His index filled 120 books! Sadly, any writer who hoped that the one copy of his book in the Royal Library at Alexandria would be a permanent **memorial** tribute to him would be disappointed. The library is thought to have been destroyed during a civil war in Alexandria around A.D. 270.

The Library at Alexandria was a great success in its time. The library and its contents were built from scratch. Books from other cultures were brought to the library. The kings would bring great thinkers of the day to the library to meet, study, and give speeches. These people were housed, fed, and paid to live there.

A scroll

More Libraries and Learning

Other libraries were built during the Roman Empire, a time when Rome was trying to take over other lands. Julius Caesar planned a **grand** library that would have both Greek and Latin sections, but he did not live to see it through. The emperor Trajan's library was established in A.D. 114. It was one of the most famous Roman libraries. It held about twenty thousand scrolls.

The fall of the Roman Empire in A.D. 476 also marked the end of its libraries. Yet libraries continued to flourish in the East, especially in Syria and Persia. The followers of the prophet Muhammad, the founder of the Islamic religion, preserved the libraries of those they conquered. Starting in the 600s, they translated the books they found into Arabic.

By the end of the 700s, Baghdad was a world center of learning. From the Chinese, Arabs learned the art of making paper from linen or cotton rags. They adopted the form of the **codex** to replace the scroll. This changed the book into the basic shape we know today. Copying and translating books preserved many that might have been lost forever during the Dark Ages of Europe.

The printing press was invented by a German printer named Johannes Gutenberg in the mid-1400s. Books were then printed rather than written by hand. As public libraries started to be built, wealthy nobles usually provided books and money. By the end of the 1500s there were libraries in almost every major European city, and many were open to the public. Valuable books were sometimes fastened to bookshelves with long chains to keep them from being stolen.

Gutenberg's printing press

Libraries in Early America

The earliest settlers of the American colonies brought some books with them, mainly for religious reasons. The wealthiest merchants and planters may have had their own libraries, but most people who could read probably only read the Bible. During the 1700s, as ways to print books improved, more people could afford to buy them, but books were still too expensive for most people.

In 1727, when Ben Franklin was a young printer in Philadelphia, he formed the Junto. It was a debate, or discussion, club. The group met once a week. They hoped to educate each other and make up for the fact that many of them could not afford to go to college.

The members of the club were interested in learning just for the sake of learning. They debated questions such as whether one form of government is best for everyone. Every three months, each member had to write an essay and read it to the whole group.

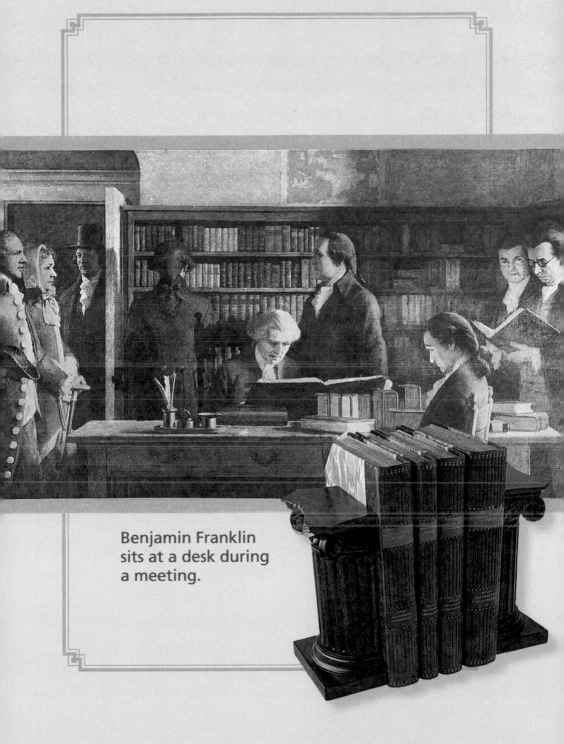

Benjamin Franklin
sits at a desk during
a meeting.

A statue of Benjamin Franklin stands
above the front door of a reconstruction
of the Library Company in Philadelphia.

Not everyone in the group could afford to have
his own personal library of books to read to prepare
these essays. So Ben Franklin suggested that the
group put their earnings together and buy books
that the members could borrow. In 1731 the Library
Company became the first lending library in America.

Fifty people gave money to the Library Company
to keep it running. By 1741 the library listed 375
titles in its catalogue. Members could borrow books
without charge. Non-members had to leave a security
deposit equal to the value of the book borrowed.

A few years later, the Second Continental Congress met in Philadelphia to write the Declaration of Independence. Nine signers of the Declaration were also members of the Library Company. In fewer than fifty years, with over two thousand books and hundreds of subscribers, the Library Company had come a long way from Ben Franklin's small debate club. In fact, the Library Company still exists today.

The idea of independent libraries eventually spread throughout the colonies and, later, the young United States. The Providence Athenaeum, in Rhode Island, was founded in 1753, and the New York Society Library was founded in 1754. In Philadelphia, the Union Library, which itself had been formed from two smaller libraries in 1746, merged with the Library Company in 1769.

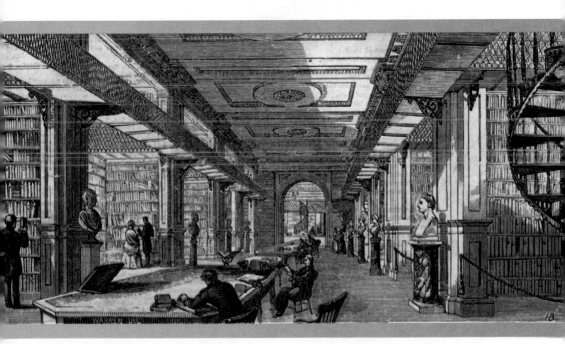

The Boston Athenaeum, founded in 1807

Carnegie the Great

In 1835, forty-five years after Ben Franklin's death, Andrew Carnegie was born to a poor family of weavers in Scotland. Andrew grew up in a small stone house with a younger brother, Tom. His father, Will, weaved at his hand loom on the ground floor. Andrew's mother, Margaret, became a skilled shoemaker. Andrew enjoyed being at home with his parents so much that he was not **positive** he wanted to go to school. He found life in his small town interesting. Andrew enjoyed hearing stories of Scottish history from his uncle, George Lauder, who ran a local grocery store.

Andrew Carnegie
as a young man

When he was supposed to begin school at the age of five, Andrew refused to go. His parents allowed him to wait until he was ready, but after three years they were concerned. They asked their local schoolmaster to convince Andrew that school was exciting.

Finally when he was eight years old, Andrew started attending school. There were 150 children of all ages in one big classroom. Though he attended school for only five years, young Andrew was an ambitious and bright student. He especially loved to memorize poetry.

As Andrew grew up, his father could not continue to support his family by weaving. Steam-powered machinery was beginning to replace hand looms. Soon work became harder and harder for Will Carnegie to find. Machine-woven textiles were here to stay. Will was very discouraged, but Margaret had an idea. Two of her sisters had already moved to America to seek a better life. So in 1848, the Carnegie family did the same. They left Scotland for the United States and settled in what is now Pittsburgh, Pennsylvania.

A Working Boy

Andrew worked in cotton mills, and he was able to work his way up to billing clerk and messenger. After a while he got a job in a telegraph office as a messenger. Soon he was supervising the other messengers, which gave him a little extra time to learn how to operate the telegraph machine. Using the telegraph, one could send messages over telegraph wires. The messages were sent in an instant through a system of dots and dashes called Morse code, named after its inventor, Samuel F. B. Morse. Once Andrew learned to translate Morse code he became a telegraph operator.

Andrew also enjoyed skating on the river and discussing current events with his young friends. He, too, formed a debate club. Despite the efforts of Ben Franklin and others, there were still very few books available for borrowing in the Pittsburgh area. There was no public library either.

One day Andrew was reading the newspaper. Colonel James Anderson, a wealthy local resident, was opening his four hundred **volume** personal library on Saturday afternoons to young workers. Andrew leaped at the chance to become a regular borrower.

The library's rules allowed only apprentices, or people learning a trade, to borrow books for free. Messengers, like Andrew was at the time, had to pay. Andrew wrote a protest letter for the newspaper. He wanted to borrow books too. His complaints were heard. As a result, any young worker, apprentice or not, could borrow books without charge. Andrew decided that if he ever became rich, he would use some money to build free libraries.

Andrew Carnegie

In 1865, at the age of thirty, Andrew had become a private investor. **Selecting** carefully, he put money into industries, including oil, iron, and steel. Eventually he created the Carnegie Steel Company, which he sold in 1901 for $480 million. Carnegie spent his life giving away more than $350 million.

One building that Andrew Carnegie funded is Carnegie Hall in New York City.

Andrew remembered his promise to create free libraries. From 1886 to 1896, he contributed almost $2 million for urban community centers that included not only libraries but also places such as swimming pool areas. From 1896 to 1919, Carnegie's gifts of money, totaling over $39 million, went to small towns to construct buildings that would serve solely as libraries.

Carnegie did not give money to every town that wanted a library. Like any businessperson, he wanted his investment to succeed, so he set specific requirements for each applicant. The town had to own the land on which the library would be built. The land had to be large enough to allow for the library to grow if needed. Most important, Carnegie required that the town pay money each year to keep the building in good repair. More than fourteen hundred towns in forty-six different states benefited from these gifts.

The Library Today and Tomorrow

Would Andrew Carnegie recognize what goes on in most libraries today? Certainly the activities of reading books, taking them out, discussing them, and returning them remain largely the same. But what would Carnegie think of using library catalogues online or reserving and renewing books by e-mail? Could he have imagined downloading materials from the Internet or sending them as e-mail attachments? What about participating in online chats with authors or discussion groups with worldwide members of an e-mail list?

These pictures show a modern library that opened in Alexandria, Egypt, in April 2002.

No doubt Carnegie would quickly see how far we have come from the days when he was allowed to borrow one book for a week from a rich man's private library. Even with his keen business sense, however, would he be able to predict what the library of our future might look like?

As exciting new technologies make it easier for people to find information, libraries will continue to help people sort through everything that is available. Libraries are more than just buildings that hold information. Libraries play important roles in our communities. They are places where people can educate and entertain themselves for free, just as Ben Franklin and Andrew Carnegie did. Libraries are places where people come together to learn, discuss, and share their knowledge. We are fortunate to have free access to these incredible places. Andrew Carnegie and Ben Franklin realized how valuable libraries were, and people today appreciate them just as much.

Now Try This

Libraries contain a lot of information for people to use. The resources found at libraries appeal to different age groups, reading abilities, and interests. Think about how your school library or a library in your community is organized, and then design your own library.

The Library of Congress in Washington, D.C.

1. Think about how would you make the library useful for local residents. Where should it be located?

2. On a piece of paper sketch out a floor plan. Where will you put the children's section? Where will people go to find reference materials to do research? Will there be a quiet reading section? What kinds of furniture will be needed? Where will you put the audiovisual equipment?

3. After you plan your library, share it with the class and explain why you made the decisions that you did. Compare your floor plans with those of classmates.

Glossary

codex *n.* an early book form with writing on both sides of the pages.

grand *adj.* excellent; very good.

memorial *adj.* helping people to remember some person, thing, or event.

peculiar *adj.* strange; odd; unusual.

positive *adj.* permitting no question; without doubt; sure.

prideful *adj.* haughty; having too high an opinion of oneself.

selecting *v.* picking out; choosing.

volume *n.* a book forming a part of a set or series.